Loneliness or Fruitful Longing

TRANSFORMATIVE WISDOM SERIES

The Transformative Wisdom Series engages the themes of spiritual, personal, and societal transformation, bringing to bear the timeless wisdom of the Eastern Orthodox Church and the cumulative wisdom of contemporary Western psychotherapies.

LONELINESS OR
FRUITFUL LONGING

Nun Katherine Weston, MA, LMHC

WESTON COUNSELING, LLC
PUBLICATIONS
Indianapolis, Indiana
2014

Printed with the blessing of His Grace
✟ LONGIN
Serbian Orthodox Bishop of the Diocese
of New Gracanica and Midwestern America

Copyright © 2014 by Nun Katherine Weston

Cover photo: the western coastline of Mount Athos
Courtesy of Hieromonk Alexii (Altschul)

About the Weston Counseling, LLC logo: The nautilus shell presents a
pattern of growth that God has used from the smallest sea creatures to
the greatest cosmic nebulae. It is a metaphor for psychological healing:
We cycle through themes, but at a greater breadth of healing each
time. The Cross is our spiritual healing. At the center of both is a pearl—
Christ Himself.

Weston Counseling, LLC Publications
ISBN-13: 978-0-692-27454-5

BISAC: REL012110
Religion / Christian Life / Social Issues

Contents

The idea dawned suddenly one November day in 2012—to write about loneliness. I would have to start from scratch. Even though I had finished a very rigorous counseling program at Christian Theological Seminary, loneliness, as I recall, was not addressed in any of my classes. Why not, I wondered…. I began to stalk loneliness as if it were a prey. What are its origins, its habits; how do we trap it and wrest it of its power? I began to hunt it in conversations, in Scripture, in books, journals, news articles, and blogs.

By the following October, I was ready to present on loneliness to the 20th annual Ancient Christianity and Afro-American Conference, a ministry of the Brotherhood of St. Moses the Black. The topic was well received, but I was not yet satisfied with the depth of my coverage. I spent the following year delving into new dimensions of loneliness and this present, modest book is the result.

Regarding the Transformative Wisdom series: You may have noticed that the third volume has been published first. The essays that I am editing and gathering, God willing, into this plus two other volumes, span a transformative, 12-year period of my own life. The first three essays, which will appear in Volume 1, were delivered as talks in the years just before I began seminary; their generous reception was part of what encouraged me to return to school. From 2003 until 2008 when I graduated, topics took inspiration from my course work. Since then, I have been writing as a professional pastoral and mental health counselor, expanding on approaches developed during seminary. Thus because of the nature of my journey, the very first essays I wrote need more editing and updating, and the later essays are being published first.

My first inspiration in the counseling field is my own mother, Miriam Drake Weston, now a retired clinical psychologist. She did counseling while carrying me in the womb, so there is little surprise that I have gravitated toward counseling myself. My second inspiration is my sister, Sharon Lockhart-Carter, a social worker, consultant, and addictions counselor.

In addition to these two inspirational women, I wish to acknowledge all the wonderful people who comprise the African Christianity Conference every year—their listening ears have elicited the essays. I am indebted to my abbess, Mother Brigid, and my spiritual father, Hieromonk Alexii for their guidance and encouragement over the years. My own St. Xenia Monastic Community has been of inestimable help—discovering off-the-beaten-track reference materials, sharing ideas, editing, and proofreading. Others who generously helped with editing and proofing are Annette Glass and Maureen Eichner. Thank you also to Theodore Nottingham who mentored me through the publishing process.

I offer my special thanks to Fr. Vasilios Thermos, Deacon Marko Bojović, and Mrs. Olga Osherov who engaged with me in conversations about loneliness; their words will come toward the end. Thanks also to Fr. Stevan Bauman and Fr. Dragan Petrović who, by their ongoing pastoral support, have played an important role.

Finally, I would be remiss if I did not acknowledge my wonderful clients who have taught, and continue to teach me so much about being human, suffering, dignity, transformation, and thriving. Here is a little story: A young boy was once overheard in church reciting his ABC's. When asked what he was doing he said he was praying—he was giving God the letters and letting Him form words of prayer. Unable to acknowledge my clients by name I am tempted, like the lad in the story, to spell out the alphabet here in large, capital letters. Thus if any of my clients should pick up this book they might pick out the letters of their name and receive it as a personal and private tribute. Thank you for helping to track down and tame the beast of loneliness.

If anything is of benefit in this small volume, then glory be to God. If anything is remiss, the fault belongs entirely to me; I ask your forgiveness.

September 10, 2014
The feast of St. Moses the Black

Nun Katherine Weston

After months of anticipation I found opportunity to visit a recently constructed Orthodox temple just outside of Indianapolis—my excitement was occasioned by a new program of wall paintings including the Pantocrator in the dome, the Theotokos in the apse above the altar and several others. The church also featured a very rare program—the creation of the world. This was painted in a circular band below the dome paintings.

This creation of the world unfolds according to the days in Genesis. On the sixth day, the energy is palpable as God the Word, appearing as the God-man Jesus Christ, blesses Adam with his right hand, and reaches toward him with his left. Adam reciprocates, reaching both hands out toward Christ in acknowledgment. But in the very next frame, Adam sits alone, looking totally dejected, head in hand, contemplating the paradisal trees. Adam is lonely. We all know how the story unfolds from there. God says: *It is not good for the man to be alone* (ISV Gen 2: 18). After offering companionship through the animals he brings Eve forth from Adam's side. Together they sin, together they are cast out, and together they sit opposite paradise lamenting.

As I gazed back and forth between the depictions of Adam's original loneliness and of his companionship in trouble it amazed me to see, at least according to this artist, how much consolation there was in the company—perhaps even more than in living alone in paradise.

The icons also depicted, with theological accuracy, the hairsbreadth difference between fruitful longing and loneliness. While Adam was still visibly with Christ he longed for his

1

Creator's presence. That longing was focused and intense. It had been bestowed upon him as an invitation to ascend above the forms of created things, so as to remain in communion with his God.

What then, was that loneliness? It was a pang for the one thing Adam did not yet enjoy in paradise—another human to relish it with, who would make him godlike by sharing in his love. Yet when that ultimate gift was also given, how foolishly our first parents sought to be godlike through the knowledge of good and evil. They had all they needed to become godlike through the opportunity to develop their mutual love.

Introduction

As crucial as this topic is, serious sociological research into loneliness began only in the 1970s. Since then the subject has drawn interest from the fields of social science, health risk, and suicide risk, not to mention existential philosophy and literature. Although loneliness is a biblical theme, as we began to explore just now, it is not a biblical word, per se. As I have shown with previous topics such as anger and anxiety, the biblical language is concrete, implying emotional states through use of words that describe behavior or circumstance.

Thus the Scriptures speak of people or nations being forsaken by God, abandoned, desolate, and without protection, but is that sense of isolation from the divine the same as the feeling of loneliness? On the other hand, the Scriptures speak God's promises that He will always be with us and protect us, but does that necessarily provide a feeling of companionship? The Bible's focus is our relationship with God and the way to restore communion with Him. The cultivation of an all-consuming thirst for God, the experience of which entails what might be called "loneliness" for God, is central to the Scriptures. The very human experience that we call loneliness—the hunger of people for people—can only be peripheral. These factors suggest to me a deeper question: Did loneliness—dejection for want of companionship—exist in earlier, communal epochs, or is it a modern phenomenon altogether?

Beginning with that question, our goal is to explore loneliness from the perspectives of community and culture on the one hand, and the Orthodox Christian faith on the other; to see where its remedies lie and how we can find strength against the forces of loneliness and atomization. Having begun with loneliness in the Bible, we will resume our exploration in the social sciences, and make our way toward spiritual reflection.

The dawn of modern loneliness

The very word, "lonely" is a fairly modern word. It was first used some 400 years ago to mean "isolated," as in "a lonely island." It was too new a word to appear at all in the 17th century King James translation of the Bible. The familiar meaning of being "dejected for want of company" is first documented in the early 1800s (OED). What was happening at that time to warrant a new meaning for this word? It was the Industrial Revolution, beginning in England and moving to the rest of the Western world.

In a nutshell, with the industrial revolution, coal supplanted wood, and machines supplanted artisans. Country people migrated to the new mines and factories for work. Cities developed rapidly around these new factories. And thus for the laborer, the time-honored rhythms of rural and village life were supplanted by the as-yet-unregulated demands of the labor economy.

This was the picture in Western Europe. But here in the United States it was compounded by an additional factor—the

European migration westward was still advancing. Young men left their homes in the Atlantic states to make a new life in the Midwest and Western territories. It was in this context of migration, urbanization, and loss of cultural matrix that "loneliness" was first named.

It is worth noting that "loneliness" is also a recent word in some of the traditional Orthodox languages such as Greek, Russian, and Serbian, although I have not been able to pinpoint the history of its entrance into other languages. Suffice it to say there is currently a lively interest in the topic of loneliness in Orthodox homelands. There will be a special section towards the end of this discussion to explore ethnic Orthodox perspectives. Having outlined the emergence of this new word in very broad strokes, let us move on to loneliness itself.

Types of loneliness

I mentioned above that the first serious research on loneliness began in the 1970s. It is credited to Robert S. Weiss, at that time Chairman of the Department of Sociology at the University of Massachusetts. In his book, *Loneliness: The Experience of Emotional and Social Isolation*, he distinguishes and explores two types of loneliness: the want of a close emotional bond—as with a parent, spouse, or child—and the want of a social network. This is an important distinction because, as he observes, fulfillment in one of those domains can still leave a person lonely in the other. Nor can a person substitute relationships of one kind for relationships of the other. (From a faith perspective, we might add that loneliness for the divine is a third, distinct type.) In the interest of coming up with a single construct for loneliness, more recent research has combined the two domains, asking about both in a single questionnaire. As a result, in this discussion a distinction of loneliness types will sometimes be discernable and sometimes not.

The feeling of loneliness

We all know the feeling—we all experience transient moments of loneliness and for some of us it is an all-too-familiar companion. But what, exactly, is loneliness? We will explore this from two perspectives—first according to Weiss's book of four decades ago, and then according to more contemporary thinkers. According to Weiss, the two types of loneliness, from emotional and social isolation, are both rooted in early childhood experiences: The first is rooted in the young child's fear of abandonment by the parents—anxiety and restlessness are prominent here; the second is rooted in the young child's experience when playmates are unavailable—boredom and restlessness are prominent here. The adult experiences are modified by adult capacities and spheres of activity, but the feeling tones are carried forward from childhood (see Weiss, 1973, p. 20).

According to today's social psychologists, and Weiss would agree, loneliness is a desire, like hunger or thirst, which prompts us to fulfill a need, in this case, for companionship. It is also a pain that comes from wanting companionship and not achieving it. Thus it often carries the feeling of rejection, shame, or failure. Loneliness evokes a certain social anxiety—it's as if the lonely person says, "I'm not good enough for other people or they would want to spend time with me." This is one of those thoughts which may feel true without actually being true—it's easy to get stuck there. The pain of rejection is not metaphorical. It is registered by exactly the same part of the brain that registers physical pain (C&P, 2008, p. 9). It can be seen on a brain scan, confirming what we have always known: Rejection and loneliness really hurt.

Research on loneliness also shows that we crave, not more friends, but deeper friendships. We crave intimacy with people who share our goals and values. Thus a person may feel isolated, even in the bosom of family, from not sharing the same value system or moral compass, or even from having a very different temperament. To emphasize the spiritual dimension, I like to say that we long for experiences of communion with others. Not just time with others, but quality time. For couples, this does not include time spent sorting out schedules and logistics. And certainly not the time spent worrying about finances.

The circle that includes what loneliness is, also excludes what loneliness is *not*. Loneliness is not grief over death or loss, although grief may certainly entail feelings of loneliness. Neither is it clinical depression or any other mental health diagnosis. It is not the same as feeling bored, although it is common enough to feel bored and lonely at the same time. For those familiar with the writings of the early Desert Fathers of Egypt and Palestine, it is not the same as the passion of acedia, although I wonder if boredom and loneliness don't play a part. After all, in the grip of acedia, the monks would go socializing when it was time to engage in solitary prayer.

What Makes Us Vulnerable?

Personal factors

FOR THE REST OF US, outside the solitary desert, what makes us vulnerable to loneliness? There are personal, social, and economic factors. On the personal level, research suggests that the tendency toward loneliness comes equally from our genes and our environment. (This is from research following sets of twins over time.) It seems that we each have an innate, genetic "thermostat" set for our optimum level of social connection (C&P, p. 14 ff). This means that whether in family groups or intimate relationships, people can be mismatched with their loved ones regarding their need for connection. People with a "high thermostat" often get messages that they are "too needy" or "high maintenance," thus being blamed or criticized for legitimate needs.

The environmental elements contributing to chronic feelings of loneliness can come at any point in life through change and loss, or early enough in our development to shape the character. Examples of the later life changes include moving to a new community and suddenly being without a circle of friends from work, church, or recreational activities. Another example is loss from divorce or death. Regarding early developmental experiences, the science editor of the *New Republic* has this to say:

> Loneliness is made as well as given, and at a very early age.
> Deprive us of the attention of a loving, reliable parent, and, if

nothing happens to make up for that lack, we'll tend toward loneliness for the rest of our lives. ... Recently, it has become clear that some of these problems reflect how our brains are shaped from our first moments of life [Shulevitz, J., May 13, 2013].

Equally important on the personal level, people with a perceived difference or stigma are more vulnerable to feeling social isolation. Their difference could be physical, mental, ethnic, economic, or even religious. They—or we—live with the daily reality of awkward encounters with mainstream society. People pretend not to notice the difference. Or else it encourages them to launch into a personal conversation beyond the normal social boundaries (see Goffman, 1963, pp. 17–18).

People with differences are also seen through the lens of stereotype. Thus, at first encounters, a whole schema of stereotype-based qualities may be attributed to them, making it difficult, if not impossible for them to be seen for who they are. A classic example of this is offering a blind person a wheelchair because of the "handicapped" schema. Or, more tragically, the shooting of a black man going for his wallet because the four white policemen thought it was a gun (Fine, C. 2006, p. 180–181).

If first encounters are fraught with so much difficulty and danger, how much more so are efforts to bridge the barriers and forge actual relationships. On the other hand, if people with differences are part of a significant group—a subculture of people like them or a group of supportive others—they may not feel particularly lonely. Rather, they may be quite able to meet their needs for meaningful companionship.

Ironically, people with actual, but invisible differences are also vulnerable to feeling isolated. This could take the form of an undiagnosed sensory or learning difficulty. People grow up comparing themselves unfavorably to their peers without suspecting an invisible handicap. Likewise they are pushed by parents and teachers to performance beyond their ability. As adults their identity has formed around this distorted sense of self, making them more vulnerable to loneliness.

Increased isolation can also come through a general tendency to put our best foot forward and to keep troubles to ourselves. Thus we can even feel isolated by thinking we are the only person suffering from loneliness when, in fact, we are surrounded by a sea of lonely people every day. That is why it's so important to talk about this.

Social factors

We have become more socially isolated by the loss of neighborly living. This can be seen by major shifts in both rural and urban life. In 1991 the US quietly passed a demographic landmark: Less than two percent of our population was comprised of farmers living on farms compared with 30% in 1920. As Wendell Berry notes: "Our farm population had declined by an average of almost half a million people a year for forty-one years" (Berry, 1995, p. 8). With this change, a neighborly life-style has been slipping away: community barn raisings, women's quilting clubs, and other like activities.

In 1949 Harry Truman signed the "Fair Deal" Housing Act. In cities across the US, populous neighborhoods, many of them quite stable, were demolished for the development of the interstate highway system or for the housing projects. In the 1950s and '60s, according to one documentary, 2,000 neighborhoods were destroyed and 300,000 families were forced from their homes by the federal government "bulldozer." About half of these families were black. Some family members were interviewed about their old Harlem neighborhood and one said: "There were eyes watching you. You could go down the street and you could count on my Aunt Bea being in her top floor window and looking out the window." A neighbor added:

"Everybody was aiming for the same thing. Everybody wanted to finish school, get a good job, help support your parents. You know, get married, have a family. It was togetherness that I cannot explain to you any better than I'm doing." Historian Richard Caro summed it up: "While these people were poor, that didn't mean they had a bad life, as long as they had their neighbor." (Epstein, J., 2011).

In an interview with Kenneth Clark for public television, writer and social critic James Baldwin described the results of demolition and dislocation, spontaneously coining the term "Negro removal":

> A boy last week, he was sixteen, in San Francisco, told me on television—thank God we got him to talk—maybe somebody thought to listen. He said, "I've got no country. I've got no flag." ... They were tearing down his house, because San Francisco is engaging—as most Northern cities now are engaged—in something called urban renewal, which means moving the Negroes out. It means Negro removal, that is what it means. The federal government is an accomplice to this fact [Baldwin, 1963].

Marc Fried did a study on working-class families displaced by urban renewal in Boston's West End. These people displayed a "strong and positive attachment to their homes and community, strong interpersonal relations and ties, and a group identity based on availability and contact with familiar groups of people." After the demolition of their community and their relocation,

> a majority of the individuals experienced the reaction Fried described as "grieving for a lost home." This grief was manifested in feelings of painful loss, continued longing, helplessness, depressive tone, and a tendency to idealize the lost place. The researcher concluded that while relocation may increase the rate of social mobility and create new opportunities for some people, for most of the working class dislocation leads to intense per-

sonal suffering, which is not easily alleviated by larger or newer apartments or by home ownership [Weiss, 1973, p. 156–157].

Whether in response to government programs, financial hardship, or personal initiative, frequent moves inhibit families from investing emotionally in their neighborhoods. Poor families move more often than middle class ones. On the other hand, better-off families may relocate to follow the father's or, sometimes, the mother's employment. These are just a few illustrations of trends that we are all familiar with, and that leave us atomized rather than interdependent and connected.

Economic factors

Economic change is a major factor promoting loneliness as well. In this age of financial transition, we suffer from a severe disconnect between what we need employment to be and models the big employers are using. That is, the employers are making demands based on the 2010s, but plan in terms of the flexibility of the ideal employee of the 1960s—the male head of the single-income household whose wife took care of the family. Companies want to keep the flexibility but not the pay standards. The effects of this disconnect are reflected in present wages, hours, and scheduling, and thus impact family function (W&B, 2010, pp. 3–5).

The past several decades have seen a shift from the "living wage" concept. Historically, some women have always worked, especially black women. However, during World War II women were drafted into the work force to replace men on the front. As women gradually increased in the workplace in the decades after the war, the expectation of the two-income family came to take precedence. As the living wage disappeared, this put even more pressure on single parents.

Now, as a nation, we are under- or over-employed. From the late 1970s until now, the average work week has gone up about 11 hours for those who work full time (W&B, p. 1), while many others are forced to piece together multiple part-time jobs without benefits to make a living. These changes not only reduce the clock time that we can spend with family and community, but create hidden costs as well. Much employment below the managerial/professional level demands employees to be available to the employer's schedule with little or no provision for childcare or eldercare responsibilities. Thus a single mother might actually work about 40 hours, but be expected to be available for the majority of the hours that her shop is open. She may only know her schedule a few days ahead. That could mean 30 or more hours a week that cannot be scheduled in advance, hindering her ability to commit to family, church, or civic activities. Presently 70% of American children live in a household where all adults work. Thus the "ownership" of their parents' time beyond the actual hours worked is a major force increasing isolation and loneliness of all family members (W&B, p. 24).

Members of working-poor families and those living on benefits face yet other types of isolation. Often relying on inefficient vehicles and watching every gallon of gas, they are not able to take their children to extracurricular activities or to pay the fees for uniforms and equipment these activities may require.

Economic and social change also results in children being kept indoors more of the time, and unable to meet up with companions for play time. Of course, latchkey children are not a new phenomenon. However, parents across the US are fearful, more often keeping children indoors because of dangerous neighborhoods or the fear of random acts of violence.

Social media

That said, American families often are hyper-scheduled, eat on the run, and communicate electronically. All these changes diminish our opportunities for meaningful social time. Here let us turn our attention to the electronic devices and the social networks. Sherry Turkle, who is considered the "Margaret Mead" of the digital age and is the author of *Alone Together* (2011), gives telling examples of how social media are not only making us lonelier, but affecting us more deeply than we know:

> I've interviewed hundreds and hundreds of people, young and old, about their plugged in lives and what I've found is that our little devices, those little devices in our pockets, are so psychologically powerful that they don't only change what we do, they change who we are [Turkle, S., 2012].

She illustrates this through an 18-year-old boy who texts for "almost everything." He tells her, wistfully, "someday, someday, but certainly not now, I would like to learn how to have a conversation...." The problem with a conversation, according to young people like him, is that "it takes place in real time, and you can't control what you're going to say." The social media allow us to edit and retouch and present the self exactly the way we want to be seen, thus sidestepping the messy complexity of in-the-flesh relationships. Being lonely but afraid of intimacy, "we're designing technologies that will give us the illusion of companionship without the demands of friendship," (Turkle, S., 2012).

There are three "gratifying fantasies" of the plugged-in life that Turkle identifies: "One, that we can put our attention wherever we want it to be; two, that we will always be heard; and three, that we will never have to be alone." These fantasies lead to a shift in the basis of our identity: "I share, therefore I am." Rather than having an experience and then sharing it, we now share as things unfold (Turkle, S., 2012). This leads to faking experiences to have something to share so that we can feel alive (Cohen, S., 2013).

As society has uncritically followed the siren lure of these electronic devices, they are being introduced into elementary schools in the earliest grades. In some classrooms we no longer see pupils watching their teacher or taunting their neighbors, but all eyes fixed on iPads. In a 2012 interview with Dr. Ruth Buczynski, Dr. Stephen Porges reflects on the developmental costs of this trend on children's ability to develop appropriate emotional regulation in the social context:

> What is the consequence of this trend? This trend results in **the nervous system not having appropriate opportunities to exercise the neural regulatory circuits associated with social engagement behaviors. If the nervous system does not have these opportunities,** then **the nervous system will not develop the strength and resilience to self-regulate** and regulate with others, especially when challenged. If schools continue on this trajectory of "technological advancement," the children will not get the appropriate neural exercises to develop an efficient neural platform to support social behavior and to facilitate state regulation. [NICABM, p. 16].

Here Dr. Porges is concerned because nature designed us to calm down from stress and upsets through the comforting bodily presence and face-to-face interaction with people we trust, who feel safe to us. If we lose the opportunity to practice this because so much of the developmental years is spent interacting with devices, we will foster a special breed of loneliness. This is not the loneliness of persons who could easily be comforted if they could find companionship, but of persons who prefer to interact with things rather than people.

The Effects of Loneliness

Physical health

ASIDE FROM A LESS SATISFYING LIFE—obviously a major concern in itself—what are the issues with loneliness? Loneliness is a major health concern, affecting both physical health and clarity of thought. It is a necessary ingredient to those tragedies where people take their own lives or those of their unborn children. And loneliness can become self-perpetuating.

Let's look at the physical health issues first. Chronic isolation poses as serious a health risk as smoking, high blood pressure, lack of exercise, or being significantly overweight. Lonely young people are no different from others in their health habits. However, by middle age, lonely adults have fewer healthy habits than other people. Among older adults "it was the subjective sense of loneliness—not a lack of objective social support—that *uniquely* predicted depressive symptoms, chronic health conditions, and elevated blood pressure" (C&P, 2008, p. 99).

Objective and subjective experiences of stressors are worse for lonely people. On questionnaires, socially satisfied adults reported fewer ongoing life stressors than lonely people. "It appears that, over time, the 'self-protective' behavior associated with loneliness leads to greater marital strife, more run-ins with neighbors, and more social problems overall." On the other hand, the personal experience of stress is more severe for the lonely even when the stressors are comparable. Lonely people also find the pleasant little social boosts of day-to-day life to be less uplifting. By way of illustration: Brain scans show that when a socially satisfied person looks at a picture of a happy face, the reward center of the brain lights up. Lonely people react less strongly (C&P pp. 102–103).

Also disturbing are the altered physiological responses to stress in lonely people. Adrenaline and cortisol, the "stress hormones," are both affected by loneliness. Cortisol, in turn, regulates immune response, including increases in chronic inflammation and even allergic responses. Loneliness even causes changes at the cellular level such that the inflammatory response is hard to turn off. Loneliness affects the circulatory system in a way that makes the heart work harder to circulate the blood and also causes more wear and tear on the blood vessels. (C&P, pp. 105–106). Finally, sleep is also diminished for lonely people. It may take longer to fall asleep and sleep is less refreshing, leading to daytime fatigue (C&P, pp. 107–108).

Just as there are stress hormones, there is also a hormone that supports positive social feelings as far-ranging as bravery and intimate connection. Peter Kirsch and his team of researchers have demonstrated in the laboratory that a substance called oxytocin reduces the experience of fear. It counteracts the stress hormones that we looked at just above and preserves or restores feelings of safety and wellbeing. It also modulates our experience of social safety versus social danger (Kirsch, 2005) and supports our ability to brave danger for those we care about.

According to Dr. David Stoop:

> What we lack when we continually experience loneliness is oxytocin, the comfort and connecting hormone. Without connection with another person, our output of oxytocin is limited. A little gets released into our system when we are eating, but its primary release mechanism comes when we connect in a deeper way with another person [Stoop, 2013].

There is another substance of interest to our topic—dopamine, one of the chemical messengers nerve cells use to communicate with each other. In the above discussion of stress, we noted that when lonely people look at a picture of a smiling face, they feel less rewarded. That feeling of reward comes from generating dopamine. According to Dr. Ward Bond, dopamine also supports feelings of love and attachment, altruism, and a smooth integration of thoughts and feelings (Bond, 2013). It supports the feeling of intense longing for a loved one (see McManamy, 2011). Low dopamine, on the other hand, brings feelings of boredom and detachment from others (see Bond, 2013). Therefore, with chronic loneliness people may be producing less dopamine as well as less oxytocin.

Does that simply reduce the feeling of loneliness to a "chemical imbalance"—too much cortisol and adrenaline and not enough oxytocin and dopamine? No, the matter is much more complex. Loneliness is also about how we think and the stories we tell ourselves about our lives.

The cognitive costs of loneliness

Loneliness also affects the way people see themselves and those around them. When people have been lonely for a long time, it affects the "executive" part of the brain. Problem solving becomes more difficult and they tend to cope in passive ("grin and bear it") rather than active ways (C&P, p. 103). That feeling of being in tune with others, being able to pick up on the shared spirit, is missing. Thus the lonely are more prone to misread social cues. They frequently become suspicious of others and are more likely to take remarks the wrong way. "One of the distinguishing characteristics of people who have become chronically lonely is the perception that they are doomed to social failure, with little if any control over external circumstances" (C&P, p. 174). Chronic loneliness leads people into pessimistic expectations and heightened feelings of vulnerability. The need to constantly be on the lookout for danger can lead to social withdrawal.

> The social strategy that loneliness induces—high in social avoidance, low in social approach—also predicts future loneliness. The cynical worldview induced by loneliness, which consists of alienation and little faith in others, in turn, has been shown to contribute to actual social rejection. This is how feeling lonely creates self-fulfilling social prophecies. If you maintain a subjective sense of rejection long enough, over time you are far more likely to confront the actual social rejection that you dread [C&P, p. 175].

On the other hand, the same set of cognitive changes— diminished problem solving and reading of social cues— makes them more vulnerable to being taken in by unprincipled people. So paradoxically, the lonely are more wary of others, but less able to detect real interpersonal danger. The result is they sometimes fall prey to exploitive people in business or professions.

People looking from the outside in may reasonably suppose that suspicious people naturally become lonely. However, the recent decades of social research on loneliness suggest the opposite—that lonely people may initially become suspicious of others because they feel hurt and rejected. Then later, if loneliness becomes chronic, they remain suspicious because of the reduced acuity in reading social cues and the tendency to take remarks the wrong way.

If you have been feeling lonely for some time, there may be a pull to use this description of loneliness symptoms as fuel for self-criticism or despair. Please fight against any such dark thoughts. If you need to, stop reading and seek out a pastor or counselor. My purpose in articulating these issues is to empower you to take arms against loneliness and the social forces that are driving its increase.

Loneliness and suicide

Thomas Joiner was a 25-year-old graduate student when his father took his own life. He went through the same shock, disbelief, sadness, and anger that anyone in his shoes would feel. But he also came to see suicide as an enemy that he could engage and conquer. He is now a psychology professor at Florida State University and has devoted the last 20 years to researching the question of suicide. In particular, given that professionals have listed as many as 200 risk factors, he asked what the common factors in any act of suicide are. Joiner believes he has the answer and has published to date three books on the topic.

According to Joiner, suicide is not an act of selfishness or cowardice as many believe. Quite the contrary, it involves a tragically misdirected heroism. Three conditions must come together simultaneously in people who take their own lives. Two of them are very common elements of the human experience, and the third, less so—let us summarize the last one first. It consists in a gradual desensitization to violence and the prospect of death. This desensitization can come through a lifestyle of risky behaviors, through sports or military discipline, or even through the practice of medicine. In this category, people have learned to suppress the body's natural self-protective instincts.

The other two conditions bear more directly on our discussion: One is the feeling of alienation or loneliness, which we have been exploring in depth, and the other is the sense of being a burden—that one's death would benefit others. (Remember the film *It's a Wonderful Life:* Hero George Bailey is in financial trouble, with few assets other than an insurance policy. "You're worth more dead than alive!" taunts Old Man Potter—that's when George concocts the plan for suicide.) With strong social relationships, we may certainly at times feel burdensome and may feel bad for needing others. But that by itself does not lead to suicide. We may feel isolated but still feel that we are contributing to the greater good. So loneliness by itself does not push a person to desperation. If we feel lonely and burdensome, but retain a healthy fear of death, or a faith-based fear of death by our own hand, we may experience a longing for death but not devise a lethal plan.

I'm about to bring up numbers, but first let us remember that each figure represents people who are living icons of Christ, not mere statistics. May God have mercy. "Throughout the developed world," according to an article in *The Daily Beast,*

> self-harm is now the leading cause of death for people 15 to 49, surpassing all cancers and heart disease. That's a dizzying change, a milestone that shows just how effective we are at fighting disease, and just how haunted we remain at the same time [Dokoupil, T., 2013].

Another perspective on the same disturbing trend: A year ago "the World Health Organization estimated that 'global rates' of suicide are up 60% since World War II" and continuing to rise (Dokoupil, 2013). According to the Centers for Disease Control and Prevention (CDC), the suicide rate among Americans between 35 and 64 years has increased by nearly 30% from 1999 to 2010 (Cassels, 2013).

While this is no comfort to the families who have faced the tragedy of suicide, overall the rates for blacks and Latinos are less than for white Americans. Perhaps being part of a minority confers a tangible feeling of belonging. Minorities, according to the article cited earlier, "are more likely to be lashed together by poverty, and more enduringly tied by the bonds of faith and family" (Dokoupil, T., 2013).

Beyond the facts and statistics, what are we to make of the growing momentum of suicide? I agree with Thomas Joiner that the most pressing need is to grapple with suicide as an enemy, redeeming lives already lost as we learn from them to save other lives. He has given us a powerful tool to understand and even disarm it. If one of his three conditions is not met, people are less likely to harm themselves. If we reach out to one lonely person, we might save a life. If we encourage a person who feels burdensome, we can save a life. We can honestly affirm a person's ability to contribute despite reduced function. For example, the sidelined and bedridden may have the time to pray for those who help and support them—no small gift of reciprocity.

Loneliness and pregnancy

In 1994 Presbytera Frederica Mathewes-Green published a book called *Real Choices,* based on actually listening to women's experiences in post-abortion groups around the country. It becomes very clear from the interviews that loneliness is central to a woman's loss of courage to continue her pregnancy. It is often a specific type of loneliness—the woman lacks any supportive confidant. Those who are close to her—husband, boyfriend, parents, or even her employer—pressure her against her will. This pressure sometimes takes the form of a threat: The baby's father will walk away, the parents will kick her out, or the boss will fire her.

A new pregnancy brings about hormonal and physical changes such as fatigue, morning sickness, and sometimes "pregnancy brain." Loneliness brings sad, empty feelings and a reduced ability to think through the options. It also brings a general feeling that others may be hostile while inhibiting the ability to recognize the real exploiters. Putting all these factors together, what is the outcome? According to a 10-year survey by Open Arms: The outcome is a hastily made life-or-death decision that three quarters of women later regret (M-G, p. 202).

Presbytera ends her book with timely observations. "The experience of pregnancy," she writes, "is about human interconnectedness at its most profound levels. We reverse the fall into loneliness by ringing the woman with circles of support." The women consistently said that "what they needed most was a steady friend to stand by them through the increasingly thicker days ahead." She encourages people to make a difference one woman at a time by being that friend (M-G, p. 175). It seems to me that this requires positioning ourselves in such a way that a woman in crisis would feel safe confiding in us before making her decision, confident that we will not judge or preach.

For me, as an Orthodox Christian, it is important not to see abortion as an "us and them" issue. I cannot afford to be naïve or complacent about abortion within a traditional church setting just because of the strictness of the teachings and standards. In its newsletter for Spring 2014, ZOE for Life! shares what the founders learned during their initial envisioning period. Care Net, which fosters crisis pregnancy centers nationwide, met with them. "They were obviously excited to talk with us, too excited," says ZOE. As Care Net explained:

> The Orthodox Christian community very likely suffered higher abortion rates than the national norm! That, they said, was due to the fact that we were not only a tightly knit ethnic group, but also a closely knit Christian organization. Our young people abort their unwanted children in order not to shame us.
>
> In disbelief, we turned to our parish priest, who sadly answered that he heard about crisis pregnancies, but in confession, when it was already too late to make a difference in the life of the child. Ask your priest and see what he has to say [ZOE, 14:1, p. 1].

Thus we see that the loneliness of being an Orthodox unwed mother can be very intense, even more so than in the general society. In addition to the common pressures that young women in that position face, the Orthodox woman, especially from a traditional Orthodox culture, may feel the pressure to protect the family name and honor very keenly. The impact of doing otherwise could be enormous and she knows this: Her parents could be blamed and shunned by others. It might affect siblings' marriage prospects. She may feel too isolated by her predicament to seek the advice of parents or pastor. The urgent question traditional Christians must answer is how to balance supporting the life of the unwed mother and her unborn child while, at the same time, upholding the Early Church teachings on the sanctity of marriage.

Taking Arms Against Loneliness

Personal struggles and strategies

SINCE THE CAUSES OF OUR LONELINESS are personal, social, economic and, of course, spiritual, it seems to me that the way out has to embrace all these dimensions. On the personal level I believe we have become acutely lonely for ourselves. In the modern world, where personal choice is looked upon as the highest value, almost deified, we fail to look at how all that choice affects us. With each major life choice we step into a new circle of belonging. As we go along, fewer and fewer of the people in these circles overlap. And we have fewer overlapping interests with people in these circles, who also inhabit many circles.

This is a very abstract description—what are ways it might play out? A woman has children by three different fathers. She has never been married, or she has been widowed, or divorced and remarried. In any case, through each additional child she has stepped into the circle of the father's relatives. Her life story and her identity embrace her relationship with all three men. But if she takes her children to visit their fathers' families, she will not likely be welcome to share the part of her life that involves the other men.

Another scenario: A man immigrates to the United States from an Orthodox homeland. When he arrives here, he chooses to join a different national church. In one circle, his adopted church, he misses the specific styles of liturgical music and iconography, the social traditions, and the special foods from home. It is hard to talk about this with his new friends without sounding critical. On the other hand, in the family circle or the circle of his ethnic group, they accuse him of betrayal.

Thus through having more opportunities for choice than previous generations, we unwittingly find ourselves engaged in unrelated circles. When we try to understand ourselves by looking into the mirror of community, it is like gazing into a fractured mirror. Each piece only reflects a portion of ourselves. So we have to find a way back to home.

Our forebears enjoyed a sense of group identity. Their sense of self was "we-based," incorporating the important familial and communal relationships. As an Ethiopian Orthodox priest once expressed it to me, he saw himself as a leaf on a big tree. His identity included the whole tree, so to speak. While we cannot manufacture that same experience for ourselves, there is something we can do: We can begin to notice how we carry within ourselves the voice and presence of people who are important to us. We might face a complex situation and ask ourselves: what would such and such a person do? This is part of our "we-based" identity. If we are distanced from parents or relatives because of past hurts, we can ask God to heal the internalized voice and image which we carry of these people. This, which we carry around inside, has become an alienated and unwelcome aspect of ourselves. If we invite God to heal this we will begin to have a fuller, less lonesome, sense of identity.

If we have been lonely for a long time and have sunk into a feeling of hopelessness about it, we may need a strategy to regain ourselves. Here are three simple steps. First, we need to learn the key "loneliness thoughts" and then to recognize them when they come. Second, we need to externalize loneliness and dialogue with it as something separate from ourselves. And finally we need to act opposite to what the loneliness thoughts suggest.

Thoughts of loneliness blame us and other people. They blame us for not being good enough; they blame others for being self-centered, ungrateful for what we do, and untrustworthy. Thoughts of loneliness tell us there is no hope for change. Loneliness tells us to isolate to avoid rejection.

We externalize these thoughts by shifting from, "I have a hard time trusting people" to "My loneliness is telling me not to trust." We shift from: "Others don't appreciate me" to "Loneliness tells me that others don't appreciate me. And do I appreciate them?" By externalizing, we can get some perspective and we can disagree with distorted thoughts.

Opposite action means that once we've identified a thought of loneliness, we do the opposite of what it suggests. Does it tell us to isolate? Then we need to take small steps to rediscover ourselves in relationship. First we experiment with extending ourselves a bit more. We begin with a "random act of kindness." Or we risk a kind word to someone as we do our errands. If we want to improve our odds for positive responses we can volunteer for a cause that really interests us because we'll meet people with shared interests. Meaningful work and activities may have the added benefit of alleviating loneliness through the very experience of engagement. If loneliness tells us to give up, we allow ourselves to "expect the best." Maybe loneliness whispers that people are "all out for themselves," still the social world is not some objective reality that we can observe in a neutral, scientific fashion. If we work to present ourselves in a warmer, friendlier manner, most of the time that is what we will get back (see C&P, pp. 237–244).

There is another approach that works with our inner feeling state. This may be useful if we just need to feel better but our situation does not lend itself to the actions described above. Or it could be a prelude—a way to work up the courage for outward action. Or again, if spouses feel lonely within a marriage or people feel lonely within a family, as often happens in today's society, this could work to reestablish closeness. This approach is to find ways to boost the oxytocin. I will address individuals first and then couples and families.

Four ideas for individuals: Fortunately our bodies produce oxytocin, not only in response to seeing a friendly face or hearing a friendly voice but also in response to memories and symbols of feeling connected. If we are able to recall and list some moments when we really felt close and safe with another person—without feeling more miserable by the contrast between then and now—if we are able to do this, we may be able to boost our oxytocin and feel a lift. Second, some people make good use of placing photographs in strategic places or saving uplifting voicemails to hear a loved one's voice whenever they wish. Third, singing together in church can boost the oxytocin. And last, but not least, chocolate is full of oxytocin. Hot cocoa or cacao nibs are both good sources—chocolate has possibilities beyond sugary concoctions.

For couples and families, a 20-second hug can boost the oxytocin for an hour or more. With several hugs a day, feelings of trust and closeness will increase. This physical closeness and warmth is a natural part of life in Orthodox homelands. When a tradition of hugs has been established, other positive activities are easier to implement, such as at least one meal together—every day if possible. Eating boosts oxytocin, and eating together even more. The Kingdom of Heaven, itself, is described as an eternal banquet at the Father's table.

If we are concerned about others who are lonely, there are also things we can do. We can help them feel safe in relationship with us by listening to what they need to express without directing the conversation to our own agenda. Rather than trying to talk them out of their fears, show them that we are dependable. We also need to remember that the living icons of Jesus Christ, our lonely neighbors, may be masked by their loneliness symptoms. We need to keep our eye on the reality of the living icon and, as an extension of that, keep lifting them up in prayer (see C&P, pp 245–246).

Social strategies

Taking arms against loneliness in the social sphere brings in the theme of the village. "Village" describes, not only a neighborhood of people, it also describes our relationship to the land, to cultivation, and to our creature friends. In this regard, Wendell Berry says: "I believe that the community—in the fullest sense: a place and all its creatures—is the smallest unit of health and that to speak of the health of an isolated individual is a contradiction in terms" (Berry, W., 1995, p. 90).

A great way to build community, and to fight loneliness, is the community garden. In 2004, a woman named Aster Bekele founded a program for young people that centers on gardening. As she says, you can use the garden to teach almost any life lesson. The program brings together Ethiopian and American children, urban and suburban youth, young and mature people. Aster approaches everything with an "expect the best" attitude and backs that up with prayer. Her program has even attracted a mention in *Time Magazine*, which reported on grant-funded programs in Indianapolis including "an urban garden created by retired biochemist Aster Bekele, where city kids explore plant science alongside Bekele's former colleagues from the Eli Lilly pharmaceutical labs" (Von Drehle, 2010).

The Fellowship of Orthodox Christians United to Serve— FOCUS North America—also promotes many sociable activities that help participants at every level to feel less lonely. The very philosophy of FOCUS combats loneliness because all people are seen as living icons of Jesus Christ. FOCUS participants include donors, staff, volunteers, and homeless and working poor Americans across the country. Among this diverse group, every interaction is seen as a two-way gift, not an occasion for self-congratulation or embarrassment.

Beyond specific programs, if we simply look for opportunities to foster neighborliness we will be on the right track. What are some qualities of neighborliness? Mutual interest and concern, reciprocity, and a sense of equity in the common good. One of the greatest challenges to neighborliness is that its demands often come in the form of an interruption to our plans, schedules, and deadlines. We have to consciously remind ourselves of our intention to be neighborly in order to welcome the opportunities as they arise. Remember the Good Samaritan.

Economic strategies

Regarding the economic solutions to loneliness, I will necessarily be brief. It seems to me that there are two possible spheres of action: The first involves social justice activism on the community or even the national scale. The other entails a review of one's own life to see if there are occupational changes that would support having more time with friends and loved ones.

Examples of social justice activism include fighting against loan sharks, lobbying for better wages, or choosing to do business with companies that have humane policies. These and similar activities could be undertaken with the hope that as people are lifted, economically speaking, above the survival mode, they will have more opportunity for meaningful connection in their lives. Those interested in social justice causes may also experience personal benefit from the opportunity to develop friendships with like-minded people.

Reviewing one's own life for possible occupational changes will not be advisable for everyone. But for those whose season of life invites transition, opportunities for meaningful connection can be one of the criteria by which to make choices. This criterion would then inform the type of occupation that was sought, the location, the schedule, and the desired compensation.

As we deal with loneliness in the personal and social spheres there will be an impact in the economic sphere. As Wendell Berry suggests: "Always be aware of the economic value of neighborly acts. In our time the costs of living are greatly increased by the loss of neighborhood, leaving people to face their calamities alone" (Berry, W., 1995, p. 20). A small or large neighborly act does make an economic difference and alleviates the loneliness of both parties.

ORTHODOX CHRISTIAN DIALOGUE ON LONELINESS

I HAVE FOCUSED, THUS FAR, on presenting loneliness from an American and Afro-American perspective. I became, however, very curious as to how loneliness was seen and discussed in Orthodox homelands. I selected three people based on their combination of Orthodox piety, education, openness to psychological perspectives, and bi-lingual fluency, and I asked them to give me their perspectives. One was Deacon Marko Bojović, a Serbian immigrant and graduate of St. Vladimir's Seminary. He is an able translator, serving as deacon at St. Nicholas Orthodox Church in Indianapolis. Another was Mrs. Olga Osherov, a Russian immigrant to Indianapolis via Australia, who earned her master's degree in Christian counseling while living there. She has many years' experience in St. Petersburg working with addicts and deprived children. The third was the Rev. Dr. Vasilios Thermos, an Orthodox priest, psychiatrist, and highly respected author living in Athens.

I began the conversation with each of them by e-mail, giving a brief background to the history of the word "loneliness" in English and asking about the words "alone" and "loneliness" in their respective languages.

This is how I posed my question to Fr. Dn. Marko:

> I am familiar with the Serbian words "sam" [alone] and "usamljenost" [loneliness]. Loneliness is a fairly recent word in the English language—do you have a sense of whether the ancient Serbian language had a word for loneliness? How was it dealt with by ancient or modern writers?

31

In response he searched the internet in Serbian and then personally gave me the gist of several relevant sites. It was he who actually introduced me to the work of Robert Weiss (the seminal loneliness researcher whom I referenced early on). Weiss, with his ideas of emotional versus social isolation, is currently being discussed in Serbia. Here is the highlight, for me, of the article on the *Zivot* website: Weiss had been researching loneliness in marriage and found it to be the main reason for divorce (*Zivot*, 2014).

Dn. Marko introduced me as well to the thought of Vesna Brzev-Čurčić, a Belgrade psychologist and psychoanalyst. She reflects on solitude and loneliness, introversion and extroversion. Solitude is a voluntary seclusion chosen by introverts. Loneliness is imposed by circumstance. For example, in a forced move to a new environment, extroverts may have fewer opportunities to be social and therefore feel lonely. She also states that it is alarming that young people all over the world are becoming lonelier than before. Some young people, she believes, act as hooligans because of feeling lonely. She believes that contributing factors to the loneliness of the young are the extension of the period of adolescence—up to the age of 25, and technologically induced passivity. (www.novosti.ru)

Dn. Marko also introduced me to St. Nikolai Velimirovic's reflections on voluntary solitude and the spiritual life. Monastic solitaries do not leave the world out of hatred for it. They wish to "stand before God" and to "look for the face of God" as it is expressed in these common monastic sayings. In the words of St. Arsenios, "I love people, but I cannot be at the same time with God and men." Psalm 68: 11 seems prophetic of the monastic vocation: *I am become a stranger unto my brethren, and an alien unto the sons of my mother* (HTM) (Pakibitija, 2014).

There were other contributions from Serbian Orthodox sources too numerous to cite. The need for solitude, not only for monastics but lay people as well, was a recurring theme. Solitude is necessary for reflection and for coping with stress. Divine Liturgy, as a communal act, is an antidote to our individualism and loneliness.

Mrs. Olga Osherov and I became engaged in an extended dialogue about loneliness. She shared with me from her perspectives both as a Russian and as a Christian counselor. As a Russian she sees that an important contributing factor to loneliness is the breaking of the intergenerational connection. People choose their own marriage partners rather than having parental input. She also brought up a topic that may be hard for Americans, especially Afro-Americans, to digest, but it has its place in Orthodox thought: The mixing of ethnic groups in marriage contributes to loneliness. Being born into a culture adds layers of depth and meaning to an individual person that outsiders to the culture will never fully understand no matter how hard they try. In marriage this can contribute profoundly to a sense of loneliness.

I found a similar theme in St. Nikolai Velimirovic's essay, "The Nationalism of St. Sava." A nation's happiness is best served by avoiding the conquest and acquisition of neighboring territories because empirical expansion will foster intermarriage. And intermarriage will bring together opposing values and worldviews under one roof, causing people to lose their peace (see Perry & Arhipov, 2011, p. 126).

Both St. Nikolai's reflections and Mrs. Osherov's harmonize with my earlier reflection on social causes of loneliness: "With each major life choice we step into a new circle of belonging. As we go along, fewer and fewer of the people in these circles overlap."

From her perspective as a Christian counselor she is interested in loneliness as a feeling of separation from God. In Western, individualistic society, people forget that God created us for His own purposes, exploring life on our own terms without reference to God's plan for marriage and procreation. This can lead to loneliness. Again, others may have committed a significant sin and feel deserving of loneliness because of that. Mrs. Osherov has spoken with other people who reported *feeling* separated from God but having no idea why. If they are believers they may interpret this as being "tested by the Lord." This third instance, she says, may be "the effect of the original feeling of loneliness which the Lord allows them to suffer in order to draw them to Himself." By this "original feeling of loneliness" I understand her to mean the loneliness that came as a consequence of the sin of Adam, when communion with the Holy Spirit was broken. All forms of loneliness are very painful, and the pain lures people into looking for earthly substitutes for divine communion. Substitutes may be self-destructive, like drugs and alcohol, or they may be benign, like pets. The important thing is to keep the hierarchy of God first, followed by people, with the created order last.

Mrs. Osherov shared the following ideas from an interview with Patriarch Kirill. Loneliness stems from a lack of an object of love. We need someone to love—whether it be another person in the flesh, or someone we carry in our heart as when we pray earnestly for that person. Loss of a love object comes when we focus on ourselves. We need to search for an object of love. And being around people we will always find someone to love, (personal communication, Jan. 14, 2014.)

Finally, I also asked Fr. Vasilios:

> I am familiar with the Greek words "monos" [alone] and "monaxia" [loneliness]. I don't find "monaxia" in any of my biblical dictionaries or text books. Do you have a sense of whether the ancient Greek language had a word for loneliness? Was it dealt with by early writers—either secular or religious?

He replied that a search of Lampe's patristic dictionary did not reveal any noun related to "monos." (As, indeed, my Bible dictionaries do not have entries for "loneliness" or even "abandonment.") Here are excerpts from his response:

"Monaxia" is really a modern Greek word. Yet the feeling is familiar in ecclesiastical literature; many psalms talk about it. Prophet Jeremy speaks about loneliness, albeit in the aspect of spiritual mission. Fathers who encourage consolation of poor and sad fellow people obviously intend to alleviate their loneliness, which adds pain to pain.

I think the feeling of loneliness is ancient but the conditions may depend on the time and mentalities. In premodern societies where collectivity prevailed, a person might feel lonely when others scorned or accused him or her, because the group's appreciation was critical for psychological well-being. In modernity, when individualism is at a peak, in addition to being ostracized loneliness may be triggered by frustration of expectation as well. Now the person is far more demanding because of needing others to share ideas and feelings, to be loved, to make partnerships, to be psychologically invested.

Let us review the themes set forth thus far in the ethnic Orthodox discussions of loneliness. In classical (and even some modern) literature, loneliness has been described by the device of evoking the feeling through the situation—without having a word for it. There is an interest in the theme of aloneness (an old word) versus loneliness (a new word). They are interested in the tension between the thirst for God and the realities of human society. They discuss the need for aloneness. They see loneliness as developing from a loss of intergenerational and cultural ties. They pursue the question of how modern trends contribute to loneliness and how loneliness contributes to modern problems. They discuss the need for love and the possibility of banishing loneliness through the act of loving, rather than the experience of being loved.

This same Fr. Vasilios, quoted above, is also the author of the book *In Search of the Person: "True" and "False Self" According to Donald Winnicott and St. Gregory Palamas*. While he does not address loneliness directly, he describes the false self as an individual who focuses too much on the intellectual side while being out of touch with the body and the true feelings. Or, spiritually speaking, the individual tries to cure the soul's sinful tendencies by "amputating" the capacity to feel, rather than learning to direct the desires toward God. On reflection, it seems to me that either position would foster loneliness: How can one be intimate with others while being estranged from oneself and one's true feelings?

Fr. Vasilios has also authored a more recent book: *Thirst for Love and Truth*. In the second chapter, he engages the thought of the French psychoanalytic thinker, Jacques Lacan. The premise is that we all carry a deep imprint in our souls from infancy of what I would call a personal paradisal experience—an overwhelming sense of multi-modal gratification as we are cared for by a loving Other who satisfies us without our having to ask for anything. " 'The desire of the Other's desire takes the form of the "desire" to "refind" the original satisfaction in which the child is filled with a [bliss] he had neither asked for or expected' " (Thermos, 2010, p. 12). In later life, as we make provision for various drives and appetites, there is a gap between the fulfillment we actually do receive and the "absolute perfect Thing" we ultimately seek, a failure which leaves us *desiring* the rest of the satisfaction (p. 13). We are unable to tolerate the knowledge that this desire has no actual, earthly object, and so, with the help of unconscious fantasies, desire takes on one form after another, each time the pursuit of it has met with failure.

> This phony staging nature of fantasy led the Church Fathers to call pleasure "deception," "image," "shadow," "sleep," "dream," "lie," etc. Real things and overt pleasures have been

donated in order to keep desire alive and with the purpose of referring to God. Thus asceticism is nothing more than an effort towards the right doses of pleasure and narcissism in balance with the right doses of limitations and frustrations; a balance aiming to rescue desire alive and unsatisfied... [p. 21].

This "desire" described by Lacan and Fr. Vasilios is the same as "fruitful longing," the destination of our discussion. Thus, while Fr. Vasilios does not address loneliness in his reflections on Jacques Lacan, I believe that one of the "costumes" desire wears is the longing for human companionship above and beyond the requirements of our nature. I have experimented with this myself: instead of picking up the phone to call someone, or logging onto one of the social media, I hold myself back and notice the *feeling* behind the impulse. It is inevitably an intense feeling of longing. If, with God's help, I am able to "rescue that desire alive and unsatisfied," I can turn it to prayer; this impulse to connect on earthly terms fades as longing finds its true Object.

Loneliness or Fruitful Longing

WE HAVE COME FULL CIRCLE. I wish to remind you of the wall paintings of Adam in Paradise, his longing for human companionship and his longing for his Creator. We also have an innate longing for others and, especially, for God. In our unpurified state, that longing for God may masquerade as many other things. In the Orthodox spiritual life we are taught to inflame and focus that longing. As the spiritual life progresses, we are enjoined to cleanse the heart from a multiplicity of desires. The heart is to focus our desire the way a magnifying glass focuses the sun's rays—enough to set a small fire.

But before we can do that, we have to be able to tolerate the feeling of longing without rushing to satisfy it with other things. Paradoxically, infants in childcare without the close, hourly presence of their mothers are expected to endure longing. (I say this by way of social criticism, not to point the finger at individual families who are caught up in the web of necessity.) Adults, however, are socially conditioned to expect instant gratification—this power for gratification is a mark of status. Rather, it should be the reverse. By having their needs easily gratified in infancy, children can mature into adults who can live with longing and pursue elevated goals.

The type of emotional balance that we need in order to tolerate longing is not taught by words, and only in part by example. It is, rather, woven into the fabric of our being through early experiences of attuned and loving care. It is imparted through a relationship with parents and caring others who are able to tolerate their own longing and who are sensitive to our feelings. Fortunately for us, our universal mother, the Church, can gently foster this capacity in us, whether our early experiences were favorable or not. She gives us a taste for it in the lives of saints, in the poetry of the Bible and the Church services, and in the counsels of the elders. She gives us practice by establishing fasts in preparation for the great feasts, especially the 40-day fasts before the Nativity and Resurrection of Christ. We can, bit by bit, redirect some of the hunger and desire for food into a prayerful desire for Jesus Christ. In the words of Saint Porphyrios:

> Christ is joy, the true light, happiness. Christ is our hope. Our relation to Christ is love, *eros,* passion, enthusiasm, longing for the divine. Christ is everything. He is our love. He is the object of our desire. This passionate longing for Christ is a love that cannot be taken away. This is where joy flows from [S.H.C.C., 2005, p. 96].

The Scriptures also show us the fruits of longing in prayer. Sometimes God keeps us waiting for an answer for a very long time—months or even years. The fervor and patience of a prolonged prayer is a spiritual fruit, perhaps as valuable as the actual gift that was prayed for, or perhaps a prerequisite for receiving the gift. Two New Testament couples famously longed for a child. They lived with that longing until they were past the years of childbearing, remaining without bitterness toward God. In time, He showed his presence and might through the miraculous conception of John the Baptist and the Holy Virgin Mary. But God was present also in the waiting.

In fact, God is present at all times and places, as He fills all in all. As the Psalmist says:

> Whither shall I go from Thy Spirit? And from Thy presence whither shall I flee? If I go up into heaven, Thou art there: if I go

down into hades, Thou art present there. If I take up my wings toward the dawn, and make mine abode in the uttermost part of the sea, even there shall Thy hand guide me, and Thy right hand shall hold me [HTM Psa 138: 6–9].

The cruel irony of loneliness is that ultimately we are never alone. It is not the reality of being alone that pains us but the perception of being alone. As I have reflected on the experience of loneliness during the last two years, I've come to realize that loneliness is not a new experience after all, but rather the pervasiveness and the intensity of it are new. The experience of being alienated in the midst of family and spousal relationships is heightened by the coldness of faith in these times—in this spiritual climate we jump about to keep warm, all the while inhaling bitter winter air.

Ultimately, our loneliness tells us that we are mortal. We will all face a moment when no earthly friend or kin can help us, when we will be alone with death.

> One moment of loneliness, at the last gasp of that fellowship with death, covers with misery a whole age of delights as volcanic ash covers a flower garden. My sweetest Jesus, be Thou the third One in my company with death, so that Thou and I remain, My Conqueror, conquer my horrible devourer, O only desired One, my Jesus, my Power and Strength [Velimirović, 2009, p. 39].

Jesus is our reviving Warmth and our most faithful Companion. Loneliness was born when we betrayed our Maker in Paradise. Loneliness is banished when we complete our journey back to Him. Just as fasting offers us the opportunity to redirect our hunger toward God, so do loneliness, and the lonely remembrance of our mortality—so fundamental to the spiritual life.

Behold, I stand at the door, and knock: if any man hear my voice, and open the door, I will come in to him, and will sup with him, and he with me (KJV Rev 3: 20). Do we recognize Christ's knock at the door of our hearts—when our loneliness is an invitation to redirect our desire, our *eros,* toward God? As we refocus on Him, our longing takes wings as a prayer for God's love to orchestrate the filling of our need. This redirection of our feelings is one of the most fundamental and powerful arts of unseen spiritual warfare. The energy is neither thwarted nor wasted, but rechanneled from the horizontal to the vertical arm of the Cross.

The Cross is not the end of the story. The Lord wishes to give us companionship and, more than that, communion—to fill our hearts with His presence. He still stands, courteously at the door of our heart and knocks. Will we leave Him there, alone?

Glossary of Orthodox Terms

Acedia: Despondency. This passion is typified by a boredom with spiritual life and a desire for distractions.

Desert Fathers: With legalization of Christianity and the end of the first age of martyrdom, zealous men and women fled into the deserts of Egypt and Palestine devoting themselves to an austere life of prayer. They wanted no worldly cares or comforts to distract them from seeking to deepen their relationship with Christ. Some of their writings have come down to us today.

Elder: In Orthodoxy, a spiritual guide and teacher, usually a monk.

Icon: Image. In the Book of Genesis, God created human beings in his icon. Icon also refers to sacred painting of the Lord, the Holy Virgin, the saints and angels, that are used as a focus for prayer.

Iconography: The art and stylistic dimensions of painting icons. There are elements of iconography that remain stable through time and across ethnic boundaries; there are other elements that are highly influenced by local custom.

Monastic: Pertaining to monks or nuns. The Desert Fathers and Mothers were monastics.

Nativity: Christmas.

Orthodox Faith: The earliest expression of the Christian faith, in continuity with Christ and the Apostles. Until the year 1054, the Eastern Orthodox and the Roman Catholic faithful were united in one Church.

Pantocrator: Almighty. In Orthodox Church painting (iconography) there are many stylistic representations of Christ the Almighty.

Resurrection of Christ: Easter.

Passion: A malady of the soul. Christ came to free us from the passions. These include gluttony, lust, pride, anger, and other vices.

Patriarch: The head of a self-governing national church in the Orthodox Faith. Unlike denominations, the different Eastern Orthodox national churches subscribe to the same dogmas and are in communion with one another.

Patristic: Pertaining to the authoritative early Church writers. A patristic dictionary focuses on a centuries-long span of Byzantine Greek rather than on Biblical Greek alone.

Presbytera: A respectful term of address for a priest's wife.

Theotokos: The Holy Virgin Mary, the Birthgiver of God.

Abbreviations

C&P — see Cacioppo, J. T. & Patrick, W.

HTM — see Holy Transfiguration Monastery

ISV — see the ISV Foundation

M-G — see Mathewes-Green, F.

OED — see *Online Etymology Dictionary*

SHB — see St. Herman of Alaska Brotherhood

W&B — see Williams, J. & Boushey, H.

References

Baldwin, J. interview by Kenneth Clark on Henry Morgenthau III's "The Negro and the American Promise." http://www. pbs.org/wgbh/americanexperience/features/bonus-video/mlk-james-baldwin/. Retrieved Sept. 22, 2013.

Berry, W. (1995). *Another turn of the crank.* Washington, DC: Counterpoint.

Bond, W. (2013). "Depression: Low dopamine, not low serotonin." *Dr. Ward Bond's Think Natural,* May 4, 2013. http://drwardbond.weebly.com/dr-bonds-blog/depression-low-dopamine-not-low-serotonin. Retrieved Aug. 10, 2014.

Cacioppo, J. T. & Patrick, W. (2008). *Loneliness: human nature and the need for social connection.* New York: W.W. Norton & Company.

Cassels, C. (2013). "Suicide rate among middle-aged Americans soars." *Medscape,* May 2, 2013.

Cohen, S. (2013). "The innovation of loneliness." http://vimeo. com/70534716. Retrieved Oct. 4, 2013.

Dokoupil, T. (2013). "The suicide epidemic." *The Daily Beast Newsweek.* http://www.thedailybeast.com/newsweek/2013/5/22/why-suicide-has-become-and-epidemic-and-what-we-can-do-to-help. html [*sic*]. Retrieved Aug. 23, 2013.

Epstein, J. (Auth., Prod., Ed.). (2011). "The tragedy of urban renewal: the destruction and survival of a New York City neighborhood." http://reason.com/reasontv/2011/09/28/ urban-renewal. Retrieved Sept. 22, 2013.

Fine, C. (2006). *A mind of its own: how your brain distorts and deceives.* New York: W.W. Norton & Company.

Goffman, E. (1963). *Stigma: notes on the management of spoiled identity.* Englewood Cliff, NJ: Prentice-Hall, Inc.

Holy Transfiguration Monastery (Trans. & Eds.) (1997). *The Psalter according to the seventy.* Boston: Holy Transfiguration Monastery.

The ISV Foundation (Trans. & Eds.) (1998). *The International Standard Version New Testament.* https://www.isv.org/bible/.

Kirsch, Peter et al. (2005). "Oxytocin modulates neural circuitry for social cognition and fear in humans." *The Journal of Neuroscience,* Dec. 7, 2005, 25 (49), pp. 11489-11493. http://www.jneurosci.org/content/25/49/11489.full. Retrieved Jan. 5, 2014.

Mathewes-Green, F. (1994). *Real choices: listening to women; looking for alternatives to abortion.* Ben Lomond, CA: Conciliar Press.

McManamy, J. (2011). "Dopamine, serotonin's secret weapon." *McMan's Depression and Bipolar Web,* June 6, 2011, reviewed Jan. 1, 2011. http://www.mcmanweb.com/dopamine.html. Retrieved Aug. 10, 2014.

The National Institute for the Clinical Application of Behavioral Medicine, (NICABM), (2012). Interview by Dr. Ruth Buczynski of Dr. Stephen Porges. April, 2012. See http://www.nicabm.com/.

Online Etymology Dictionary (OED). http://www.etymonline.com/.

Pakibitija. (2014). www.pakibitija.com /index.php?option=com_content &task=view&id=124&itemid=78.

Perry, M. O. & Arhipov, S. D., (Eds.). (2011). *The new Chrysostom, Bishop Nikolaj Velimirović,* (Sr. Mikhaila, Trans.). New Canaan, PA: St. Tikhon's Seminary Press.

Shulevitz, J. (2013). "The lethality of loneliness." *The New Republic.* May 13, 2013. http://www.newrepublic.com/article/113176/science- lone-liness-how-isolation-can-kill-you#. Retrieved Sept. 23, 2013.

Stoop, D. (2013). "The brain of a lonely person," *Marriage and family matters* blog posted Sept. 10, 2013. http://drstoop.com/ the-brain-of-a-lonely-person/. Retrieved Oct. 24, 2013.

Thermos, Fr. V. (2002). *In search of the person: "True" and "false self" according to Donald Winnicott and St. Gregory Palamas.* Montreal: Alexander Press.

Thermos, Fr. V. (2010). *Thirst for love and truth: Encounters of Orthodox theology and psychological science.* Montreal: Alexander Press.

Turkle, S. (2012). "Connected but alone?" *TED Talks.* Filmed Feb., 2012 and posted Apr. 2012.

Velimirović, St. N. (2009). *Akathist to Jesus Conqueror of Death.* Safford, AZ: St. Paisius Monastery.

Von Drehle, D. (2010) *Time Magazine.* Thursday, July 22, 2010. Retrieved from: http://content.time.com/time/magazine/article/0,9171,2005863-1,00.html.

Williams, J. & Boushey, H., (2010) "The three faces of work-family conflict: the poor, the professionals, and the missing middle." http://www.americanprogress.org/issues/2010/01/pdf/threefaces.pdf. Retrieved Sept. 27, 2013.

Zivot. (2014). www.b92.net/zivot/novodoba.php?nov_id=420060.

Made in the USA
Columbia, SC
07 July 2023

20153552R00038